Divine Nature

Of
Being

Poetry From
The Flame
Of Devotion

By The Muse Of
Donna Still

Cover Design: Donna Still
Book Design: Donna Still www.donnastill.com
Book Production: Create Space an
www.amazon.com company

Legal Disclaimer

This book is presented and designed for the sole purpose to provide educational information and motivation for our readers. Whilst the best efforts have been used in the preparation on this book, the author and publisher make no representations or warranties of any kind and assume no liabilities of any kind with respect to accuracy or completeness of the contents and specifically disclaim any implied warranties of merchantability or fitness of use for a particular purpose. Neither the author nor the publisher shall be held liable or responsible to any person or entity with respect to any loss or incidental or consequential damages caused, or alleged to have been caused, directly or indirectly, by the information contained herin. Every situation is different and you should always seek the advice of an experienced professional practitioner before embarking on any self-improvement program or soul journey.

The Divine Nature Of Being

Poetry From The Flame Of Devotion

By The Muse Of Donna Still

Dedicated to you dear reader
And all that you can be,
Follow your heart and lead with love
always.
Thank you for your creative flow.

Contents

Introduction

This book contains a selection of poetry brought through by the muse of Donna Still while in deep meditation. I feel deeply honored and humbled by the creativity that has shone and continues to shine through the words contained in each poem. It feels like a true revealing of the soul within, my soul or the one soul that is always waiting for an opportunity to burst forth and blossom.

Over the past 18 months I have been on a great adventure with the divine creator that has become accessible through a combination of connecting with amazing individuals who inspire me to live from my truth, ancient breathing practices, music & plant medicines. The divine within is accessible to each and every one of us when we choose it.

Each poem contains both mystery and instruction on how one can become closer to knowing the divine mystery within that operates in and through our world by many names. You may know this mystery as the creator, the source, the essence, the soul, god or Great Spirit. I believe that all these terms are words describing the same phenomenon that can only be experienced. We all have moments in our lives where we are at one with the all that is. We all have access to it in the moments when we are completely lost in the beauty of a single flower. Or when we are totally engulfed by a small child's gaze, as we look deeply into their eyes we have the capacity in that very moment to experience the totality of all that is. I know I have had these very experiences with our grandchildren.

Through out the content I have made an effort to place annotated 'Notes:' These are places where I felt called to write additional information about what was happening or revelations I had at that moment in time.

My intention for publishing these poems from the flame of devotion is to share the beauty and serenity in connecting to the deep, deep wisdom we each contain within. To share the struggles and the triumphs of what it has taken me to liberate my own soul and feel into the fullness of love.
To offer an insight into my personal life initiations and how when we step back and look at the bigger picture we can see just how everything is connected and for our highest good.
And how in those very moments when we felt we were at the very edge of our snapping points inner resilience is born, strength and courage is developed. Becoming insights, strengths and blessings beyond our wildest dreams, all from trusting in our journey of life and living.

Heartfelt Thanks and Deepest gratitude

Before we get into the juicy yumminess of the poems I would like to give thanks in deepest gratitude for the people I admire most for their incomprehensible contribution to my life and the continued impact they are still delivering to the lives of many others.

Firstly deep gratitude to my husband and partner for the past 26 years Alan Still.

Offering my deepest thanks to Rita Hraiz for her commitment to birthing the awakening process in all that are called to sit with her in sacred ceremony for life. Kauhtli, for sharing ancient prophesies and shamanic stories that will inspire me for years to come.

Ram Dass for sharing his struggles and highlights on how important it is for us to, 'be here now.' And that everything is 'grist for the mill,' in our awakening journey.

Darpan, The Blue Lions, Snatam Kaur, Ayla Schaffer, Shrinari – Lucidia & Raphael, Peruquois and Danit for their amazing musical contribution that speaks deep into my soul.

Gabriel Icka Martinez for being the light connecting the divine masculine and feminine within and showing me how from that place of pure connection, creativity explodes forth, free from all constraints.

Rachel Elnaugh for being a light to prove that it's possible to build a business around ones dharma.

Joanne Elliott for her amazingly honest friendship.

Judy Piatkus for her very interesting conversations on consciousness at the conscious café. And finally sincere love and gratitude to Lily Ava for letting me know that I had a duty to share these words with the world. For that I'll be forever grateful. ☺ x

Radiant Expression

I'm so tired of the games
Living lies that perpetuate the cycle of
external authority
I hear the calling from within to live
from my hearts true purpose.

The purest love changes everything
Revealing the truest self expression
Love changes everything
I am a radiant expression of love.

The inner beauty of all that is
Waiting to burst forth from creation
The mother
She loves you in every expression,
Waits gently to caress you and
Welcome you back home.

The purest love changes everything
Revealing the truest self expression
Love changes everything
I am a radiant expression of love.

Letting go of the games liberates you
To begin Living from truth
Your most inner most radiant expression
of love

The purest love changes everything
Revealing the truest self expression

Love changes everything
I am a radiant expression of love.

As we release the past and
Stop looking to the future,
We notice the present
Such beauty within each moment

The purest love changes everything
Revealing the truest self expression
Love changes everything
I am a radiant expression of love.

Freedom
Liberation is complete
All past dissolved into radiant love
The purest love changes everything
Revealing the truest self expression
Love changes everything
I am a radiant expression of love.

Deep Inside

Deep inside
There is a burning
A yearning
A connection to the earth
That burns in everyone

Kindle that fire
Let it rage
Until it fills every cell in your body
With the passion and the love of your
truest expression

The creator she loves you
Waiting patiently for you
To realise this deep soul full connection
Has always been

Great mother
She welcomes you gently
Into her arms
Comforting and nurturing
Your very being

Pachamama I'm home in your arms
You are so deep in my heart, in my cells
Loving all that is
As the fullest expression of truth
Deep inside we are one
I surrender all that I am to you
To the totality of all that is this life

Note: I wrote this as a prayer to keep me on the path
as I struggled letting go of the illusions within. To act
as a bridge from judgment to grace

The Shining Self

Lord grant me the grace to see thy love in
all
To be free from fear and greed
To be free from anger and self will

Lord grant me the wisdom to feel thy love
In every act, free from limitations of my
past conditioning

Lord grant me the grace to transcend this
duality
To become an instrument of your will
To live in the infinite love of thy shining
self
The self that is one with all

Lord grant me the wisdom to
KNOW WE ARE ONE IN ALL
And the radiance of your love is always
present

Note: As I surrendered deeper into trusting my inner guidance I began waking up early hours of the morning with song lines in my head and heart. Initially I fought with them trying to go back to sleep but they were so persistent, at 2am I sat up and wrote the next three offerings then went back to sleep in total peace. This has since been a regular occurrence in my life. I no longer fight with my internal guidance; I just act immediately on the inner guidance received. It has always turned out for my highest good.

Surrender
Woman of the universe
Woman of the earth
Lover of humanity

I am you and you are me
The earth moves and I am free
Unto thee we walk the path
To deliver humanity
Surrendering

Dissolving the fear
Dissolving the pain
Offering it back into the earth

Burning inside
Where pain once resides
Like a lover, my beloved
We walk this path together

All in one and one in all

17

Truth the only constant
Love the only guide

Bringing compassion
Lightness of touch
Caressing my heart
With such joy and purity

Connect into your heart
The divine source is always inside
Let go
Trust, Trust, Trust

Note: For many years I really struggled with being in this physical body. The struggle was greater when I was younger because I could see how different it was for boys and girls. I was a tomboy, climbing trees and doing things that girls just don't do! It was the late 60's early 70's and I saw how men treated women and it wasn't always very nice to witness.
We lived in a ground floor council maisonette in Swanley, Kent and above us lived a couple with small children. The man worked away and the woman never really went out on her own anywhere. When he was home there was always a lot of screaming and shouting from him, bashing and crashing around and even using physical violence to control the woman. My mum would always call the police out of a sense of morale duty but in those days nothing ever changed and he was never charged. To add to this my uncle also physically abused my aunt, every one knew it, but nothing was ever done. I found it very hard to

comprehend why these people stayed together. I never understood the depths of the psyche then or the devices we use to cover up the truth and lie to ourselves. I realise now it was witnessing and experiencing these types of events growing up that has led me along the path I am now on. My early hatred for my body and being a woman manifested a series of physical events that would mean I would eventually have the internal organs of womanhood removed from my body at the age of 32. I had a condition called Endometriosis and required a hysterectomy initially and then at 36 with large grapefruit sized cysts on my ovaries they were also removed. Every internal part that marked me as a woman was now removed and still I wasn't free of the deep hurting inside that caused the initial wounding. On reflection I realise that the real issue was a lack of acceptance within of both the divine feminine and masculine energies. I was totally confused and lost but wasn't consciously aware of any of it. Which is why I began sharing these deep insights with the people in a facebook group called Healing The Mother Wound.' This group is all about helping each of us to stand in our authenticity and own each part, now. To stop hurting ourselves unconsciously and begin the journey of deeply nurturing each other by reuniting the divine feminine and masculine within. It's only when this happens that we can truly step into being all that we can be.

This next poem is really about reuniting the lost, broken and forgotten parts of the divine feminine and masculine within me while in this physical incarnation. In a deep reflective retreat with the Grandfather spirit of fire I remembered and became aware of all the times I had 'forgotten' that I had been deeply supported and nourished by the masculine presence in this lifetime. This realisation led to a deep healing within, the following two poems reveal the deep emotional healing that took place in front of a sacred fire.

Union

My beloved
Lover of woman
Lover of the divine
Lover of the deep radiance of the earth
(Keeps me warm)

Pure essence of love
Purest expression of truth
Divinely guided by hearts true desire

Connecting each cell
Removing the veil
Unfolding
Becoming
All will be revealed

Like the sensuous lover
The true divine union
Releases the heart
To fully, radiantly express
The truth of the universe

Complete
Being love

Liberation (I love you)
The loving union of the fire and the earth
burn deep in my body

Prayers for dissolving the pain of the past
take me through
The deep layers of my struggles

Dissolving them, releasing them
Allowing them to be free

Returning to the mother
The glorious lover
To feed me and nurture me
The way she has for millennia

Mother how I love you
Great mother how I know you love me

As this loving union of the fire and the
earth unite in my body
Taking me to the deepest parts of my
heart
The inner universe

Brining forth love
Bringing forth lovers to collaborate freely
Returning to the mother
Waiting patiently
Silently
For the time to come

When surrender is the only true path

Surrendering thy will
Completely liberated and free
Stepping into my body

Returning to the mother
The glorious lover
To feed me and nourish me
The way she has for millennia

Mother how I love you
Great mother how I love you
I love you
Thank you
Thank you
Thank you

Note: The more I've attended retreats, taking time to really look within, I've been blessed with the opportunity to work through each layer of my identity built around unconscious decisions made in my early life, I've begun to understand what a great adventure life really is. What amazing opportunities for growth we are presented with in every moment, if we are awake enough to see them. In the Language of Emotion by Karla McLaren, major or traumatic events are referred to as initiations or rites of passage. When major events in our lives are treated in this way they become great learning tools for our development in my experience.

Great Adventure

Dreaming awake this turbulent turquoise sea lashing around me, drowning the me I see in the mirror, pulling me in, closer and closer,
Do not resist
God, I surrender, they will be done
Take me from this dream
As your servant,
Please guide me,
No need to remind me who I am or what I'm here to do any more
I'm a child of light and here to do your work

I hear you through my senses
Willingly deliver
What ever you ask of me

Kundalini energy rising
I'm awakening deep into my heart,
I see you at work in every
Little detail
All perfect as it must be for
I am
All ways connected above and below
I am a complete and open vessel
I am open to receive blessings of universal
energy,
Living in right action
Loving every moment,
In the peace and calmness of being

Travelling deep inside
On this great adventure
Revealing the divinity
Of each individual
As one facet of the fractal whole
Infinite and free,
Unbounded,
Full of joy,
Full of love for what is.
Om shanti shanti shanti

Note: A topic that has really fascinated me over the years is people and what drives them to do what they do in the way they do. In fact it eventually became an obsession for me, but one that I was never fully in control of.

For many years I genuinely thought I was stupid. I didn't believe I had any special talent or gifts. In fact I was very ordinary. I left school with low grade CSE's and just got a job like everyone else. Growing up I heard a lot of, "you'll never amount to anything." The problems continued because I couldn't keep the jobs very long. Sometimes I would last up to 12 months and other times less than 12 hours that was until I had children.

Then everything began changing. I worked as a night care assistant from age 22 until in my early thirties. During that time quite by chance a mum at the school mentioned a course that was aimed at getting women in the construction industry.

So while working nights and despite having 4 children between the ages of 2 – 8 I retrained as a painter & decorator. I loved the autonomy, the creativity and most of all the freedom it gave me financially. It was truly the first time I had become financially independent. It fitted perfectly around the kids and I was my own person, growing daily in confidence. Or so I thought. As time passed I decided to add further skills to my repertoire such as interior design. I believed it would really add to my professional practice. The tutor we had Tomris Tangaz, totally changed my life. She was much younger than me and saw something in me that I couldn't see in my self. She recommended that I apply for a BA hons course at Chelsea College of Art and even filled in all the forms etc. Making me sign them when she had finished. I never believed for one minute that I'd be accepted. On the day of the interview I managed to get on a bus going 30 minutes in the wrong direction. That was some serious self-sabotaging and I had no conscious Idea why. Once I realised I was going in the wrong direction I got on a bus going the right direction and arrived over an hour late for my appointment. I never made any excuses; In fact the receptionist at the college gave me a perfect story without any of my input. I wasn't really present in the interview because in my head I had already blown it, so what was the point?

To my shock and horror I was offered a place on the 2 year fast track degree course studying Interior & Spatial Design BA (hons) Those two years were the most testing of every ounce of perseverance, inner strength I had. Somehow I got through it with a lot of help from friends and family. In fact what happened was nothing short of a miracle. I no longer felt stupid! I was good enough but of course I was still so unconscious then about what was driving my behaviour. I went on to do 2 years further study in Architecture & Interior Design, MA (RIBA Pt2) choosing finally to go back to my comfy decorating practice. I worked freelance for a while in Architects practices but decided I preferred the non-office environment. Not enough autonomy for me.

I realise now that for many, many years I've had an inner calling or yearning to be free. To not be constrained by 'others' opinions. To not be fitted into a box but have struggled to articulate just what it is. After having had what is now termed as a 'Portfolio' career I'm in the perfect position to finally understand how each of those opportunities placed in my way were massive opportunities for growth and development or initiations. I can quite easily say that none of these experiences was easy when in it and I spent a massive amount of time crying in despair but something, somehow drove me through all that inner and outer turmoil. I believe it was the years of hearing, you'll never amount to anything, and you can't stick at anything for more than five minutes, from family members and schoolteachers.

All proving to be such an intense driver to prove myself, not to be flaky, not to give up easily on myself and to keep on, no matter what to find a way. One of my mantras for life has been that anything is possible, I just need to find the way by being open to all possibilities. Quite often as Joseph Campbell said, "The cave we fear to enter holds the treasure we seek." The next poems are about diving fully into surrendering any notion of being the driver. We are all internally driven by our past experiences, that makes us more the spectator whether we realise it or not. Opportunities regularly come cloaked as challenges containing the seed of potential to be our biggest opportunity, our job is to let go and know that the universe has our back if we let it.

I Hear You

As I pound the shores of my mind
I hear you
Calling me to be free
Leave behind the comforts and follow
your hearts desire
No more hunting
No more clinging
There is so much you don't see
Cultivating loving thoughts
Frees and liberates you
Following your heart
You will always be free

I hear you calling me to my familia
Answering my prayers
Reuniting with my tribe
Being at peace in this world
Full of love and support

I hear you calling me
Manifesting my dreams
Abundant in this moment

I feel you touching my heart
In ways that'll never part
I hear you

When I Surrender

When I totally surrender to the divine
within everything works out the best way
possible.
I realise even though I have a mountain
of tools that helped me get to this place in
my life I now know everything comes
from within.
Everything for this exciting next stage in
my life can only come from within fueled
by my connection with the divine.

Meditating, I realise there is no
separation,
No difference between you and me,
Being one, being all.
Loving what is, dissolved into this union,
no longer separate
Loving what is, dissolved and
surrendered in loving service

Being internally called by the mother to
live free,
To live complete in liberated, loving
service
Following my inner knowing, the guiding
light of my soul
Glowing and growing in courage to trust
my inner knowing to guide my way home
When I surrender to the light of my soul I
am home, I am free, I am, I am

Note: So many exciting things have been happening in my life since I began to fully surrender in service to humanity. There are no longer any internal struggles or wrangling but there are plenty of opportunities for discovering all the places I had been using to hide and stay small. For example I recently completed a contract teaching a group of 16-20 year olds in painting & decorating (that's my trade background) So many smokescreens were revealed to me, the only way they were recognizable was because these were the ones I had used all my life! Projection is the device or shadow we use to hide. Whenever we recognize a behaviour in someone else that we find irritating it's a sign that we have found yet another disowned part of our true selves. The easiest way I found to bring the parts back in was to look for areas in my own life where the same thing was happening. For example one of the lads created a lot of drama that prevented him from participating in activities if he thought he couldn't achieve the required outcome. Rather than fail he wouldn't even attempt the task. At first it was puzzling to me, but when I recognised where I had been doing the very same thing in my own life, it stopped! The reason it stopped was because I took responsibility for changing it. I thanked that part of me and asked what it required to feel satisfied it would be ok. I've been doing this in depth inquiry for over 20 years and still I'm amazed at what I find hiding and the simplicity of what is needed for success.

Diamonds

As I live this life
As I walk this path
The truth of love shines bright
The miracle of love is strong in my heart,
guiding me deeper into
The truth in all ways.
Loving what is shows me how to be free in
this world.
Surrendered and true,
One heart
Living from truth
We are all creations of the divine
Diamonds sparkling
The clarity of light shines in our dark
moments, liberating the truth, releasing
the light within.
We are diamonds sparkling, let the truth
be known.

When fear no longer lives
Freedom reigns
When I surrender, I see truth
We are diamonds sparkling with light,
brilliant and bright

Drop into your heart and feel the light
Let it carry you to places of hearts delight
Free and child like
Innocent and free
When I surrender I see

We are diamonds sparkling with light,
the light of all beings

Facets revealing the beauty within
Facets revealing, loves wing
To carry you places making
Your heart sing
Full of beauty and truth,
All that is within.
We are diamonds sparkling within

Passion of love, passion of light
Journey to the center,
The diamond within
Allow the revealing
The true healing
The truth,
*We are **all** diamonds*
Sparking within

The beauty is breath taking if we take the
time to see
Seeing is a choice, we get to make
Using our will to direct our attention to
the light within
No more distractions
Allowing the light to sparkle within
We are diamonds sparkling with light,
the light of all beings
I am a diamond

Sparkling with light,
The light of all beings

Note: I dedicate this next poem to Lily Ava, beautiful sister who encouraged me to publish these deeply felt poems, telling me once that, "I had a duty to share them," thank you for your presence, your being and your light, may it forever shine bright.

Release Your Wings
Life's too short
To get stuck in struggles
Too precious to worry about
Stuff you cannot change
Find your purpose
Release all that holds you back
Look for the passion
You hold within
Lead with love
Share your gifts with the world
The creator endowed you with wings that
you may fly
Let go of worry,
It no longer serves your purpose
Let go of fear,
That's the old paradigm
Live free
Be
Alive with love
For every thing and every one
Use your story
To change your world
Fill it with love
Compassion

Heart centered truth
Shines from every cell
Radiant
Release your wings and fly
Aho, Great Spirit

Note: learning to trust ones inner guidance is the key to freedom and liberation is this lifetime. True liberation comes from within; it's not something bestowed on you by another; It's a process of little steps or big strides that reveal more and more of your true self.

We all have a gift, something that marks us out as special but sometimes don't recognise it because we have learned over time to not trust it, maybe because it comes so easy to us. Or, it may have even got you into trouble and you have been struggling with it.

In my experience when others haven't understood what I'm saying or doing, to cover up their feelings of insecurity or feelings of stupidity they project it and do their best to cover up by making me wrong. We each have the power inside to know and speak our truth. Trust it. Never, ever let anyone else tell you otherwise.

Let Go And Know

This river runs fast
And sometimes my fingers hurt
Holding on so tight
I wish I could just let go and know

Every action is guided
Every word is blessed
With the light of liberation
If we only we could let go
And know how to see it

Letting go of the past
Allowing new opportunities
To grow in this sodden earth
Tears of sadness morph into tears of joy
when we learn to let go and know

Every event is perfect for our initiation
Perfect for planting the seeds of change
Expanding our boundaries
Beyond the known
Creating and birthing
From deep within

If only we knew the beauty already
We inhabit a vast and wonderful world,
Full of awe-inspiring beauty

Removing each layer
Brings harmony within

When we develop faith to surrender
Letting go of knowing that
Hidden behind The veils of my mind,
Circumstance no longer reigns
Further Deepening into the
Beauty within

Daily practice of surrender cultivates
spring in this garden of self-love
Planting more seeds of love
Delivers a harmonious bounty
When we let go and know

After the blossom
Abundant fruit naturally follows
Becoming the beauty we see within
Each new root
Grounds us in presence
Each new root
Grounds us in love
For sharing our beauty within
As we let go and know

Harvesting the full ripe moments into
blissful states pure
Wisdom keepers reveal their secrets as we
tend our garden within
When we let go and know

Truth Of The Ages

When we go down to the banks of the
river
We can release our tears and fly
When we release our tears and fly,
Spirit shines through with such brightness
Previously blinded to the truth of
Who we are
As our insight grows,
Our hearts glow with such intense love
that we forget the illusions
Leaning further into the light,
I finally understand
I am free
I am the light and the dark
I am love and peace
I am in all and of all

This is the truth of the ages
That all great sages
Have taught us
As I radiate my love,
As I radiate my truth
I shine bright and become love
Loving all brothers and sisters
Loving all nations
We are all one
In the name of love
Re connected to the divine essence
The source of all life

Cosmic Soup

In this ocean of life I find
I'm walking without overthinking
Living from essence that pours through
every cell
I love this gentle way of being
In this lifetime
Living from love and
Consciously choosing
In every moment
To be of great service
To humanity

Inside this cosmic soup
I find I lost my mind
Acting from instinct
Guided in my actions
By a calling deep within
Dissolving
Into the fire of awareness
We are always perfect in the eye of what
is
Defenses depart
In courageous acts
No more enslaved by
Unfulfilled fantasies
Seeing truth beyond
Liberated and free

Guiding Me Home

All things are caused by imagination
Using our blissful states we can bring any
thing into being
Imagining, intensely, influencing all those
who can help us realise our dreams
It works for everyone and all
The ancestral soul, calling and guiding
you to your ancestral home
Hearing the voice within getting louder
and louder
Every day surrendered in service
Deliberate decisions in love with the
creator
Every act dropping ever deeper and
deeper into my heart
Loving the beloved, surrendered and free
Loving the beloved, liberated yet present
in every moment
Only love brings me home in my
ancestral heart

Note: Inspired by the headlands of the estuary of the Bristol Channel and the Taff Estuary while holidaying at the beautiful Welsh Village of Laugharne, the home of Dylan Thomas It was a rainy misty day where the banks of the estuary were barely visible, that's when I noticed the land opposite looking like a body laying in the mists at the waters edge.

ı *Release*

As I lay here with the sound of water
gently lapping around my head,
I release
I release the struggles of the past and
Fear of the future told
Holding my presence in this moment
clear and calm
Even though the tempest calls me with
every breath
I choose to lay calm
Under the stars clarity and opportunity
comes and goes
I begin to find my flow just laying here
letting it go
Passing by
Like clouds of mist
Releasing into the depths of my being
No longer seeing or judging
What's right or wrong but
Finding a way to
Love it all
I release

Glow

Opening the door to the creator
This flow immense
Sometimes so full
Allowing the intensity
To course through my body
Energizing and healing me from within
all the hidden places
Changing the very structure of being
More a spectator than doer
A circle of light surrounds me revealing
deeper and deeper layers of potential
Wisdom within out flowing,
No point resisting
As the soul of my heart releases the bonds
and begins to soar with the eagles
I see far and wide the positive impact I've
had
On the lives touched
I notice how that feels inside
Every thing perfectly played out as
planned
A warm glow knowing
Surrendered into the void

Earths Heart Beat

Pachamama, when I'm with you I
dissolve
Deeply surrendered into your strength
supported in all ways
Each lunar cycle I grow into wholeness
supported by your purity, your essence
pulsing through my veins
The pureness of your truth
Calms my mind
As I harmonise in oneness,
Liberated by breathing
The unity and freshness of
Our connection
One channel in
Loving service to humanity
The simplicity electrifies me to
Deliver with total presence
Being one divine channel
A prayer for you pachamama
I do it for you because
In your service
I am liberated and free
Connected by our earths hearts beat

Moments

My heart is exploding with
Love for all things
The beauty I see all around every day
How simply the heart wishes to be.
Those quiet moments where we lose our
mind and become intoxicated by the
sheer beauty and presence of a flower
Liberated and free
That's where we are all one in the
universe
Being one in both worlds
The real and unreal
The seen and unseen,
Traversing both with ease
We reaslise there is no duality
Even when we forget our connection
The creator breathes through me,
Together we are liberated and free

Dreaming Awake

As I surrender into new ways of being
bridging two worlds
Dreaming awake
Divining the tools to walk
Gently on this earth
Becoming the channel
Inspiration coursing through
Guided by source
Loving all that is

This journey to the center
True self begins and ends with
This physical incarnation falling
Into the cosmic void
Where everything is no thing,
And no thing is everything
Each part contains the whole,
The paradox of life

Conscious evolution calling my soul
Becoming limitless is the goal
The divine essence within
Diving deeper and deeper into the
creative powers within

Every experience a jewel
Beautiful, colorful gifts
Radiant, Shining to become
The very fabric of life
Aho

Respect

Deep integration flowers
From deep introspection
How astounding
Full of love and appreciation
For all living beings
Knowing my destiny is to share the word

The situations and scenarios
Repeat until we complete
Developing the strength within
To clear the past karma
Experiencing intense joy for each
Juicy moment
Patterns no longer repeated

Broken open
At the feet of such
A humbling great wisdom teacher
The true self is always available
"We live not by the breath that
Flows in and out
But by him who causes the breath to
Flow in and out"

We are not our bodies,
We are the fire,
The sun, and the light
We are the earth, and the darkness
We are pure divine consciousness,
Always connected to source

Always able to discern right action
With love and respect in our heart
For all that is
Everything is always available to those
who know

Dissolve Into Love
Supported by love
Silent storms
No longer rage within
Uniting the thunder and lightening with
the rain of passion
Your love washing me clean

Waking up from this dream
Realising for the first time that
I'm not the one in control
Letting go of drama and illusions
All is revealed

How easy it is to get lost
In the being someone
Somebody-ness creates great stress
Dissolve into nothing
And you will become
Everything
Free your mind
Knowing you're always protected,
always guided
Everything is for the highest expression
of your true self

Love wells up from deep within
Releasing the love for all
Brothers and sisters
Life becomes a living prayer.
Every

Sacred
Step,
Every breath
Giving thanks to the creator
For all love freely shared
In this body at this moment
Liberation tastes so sweet

Knowing the beauty of light
Always available,
Whispering
Calling us home
Whenever we open our hearts
Our minds,
Becoming present

Be gentle with yourself,
Your body, your being
Revealing the true beauty within.
The beauty within has always been
Now you can see it,
Feel it,
Sensing your way through
In the light of love

Loving what is
Dissolving all fears,
Absolving all pain and grief

I surrender my life to you,
The Great Spirit

Guide me
I hear you calling all day
And all night

As I listen to the music
That lives in my heart
I feel you inside me
Gently guiding my every action
Great spirit
I am totally devoted,
To live by your will
I love how you feel deep inside me
I love how you abide within me
I dissolve into love

Note: I dedicate this next poem to Gabriel Icka Martinez, divine brother ji. We connected at a sacred medicine retreat during the summer of 2016 and have spoken almost every week since.

Warrior

Warrior of light
Warrior of truth
I surrender into the depths of your being
I dissolve into the nothing to
Become everything
Serving only truth delivered via our
divine connection to the
Wellspring within of wisdom pure
Becoming a unified channel
Revealing the light
Unfolding the petals
Supporting and nurturing the beauty
I see all around me
Touched by the presence that
Is always available
Guiding me home to my heart of
Light and love within
Oh, warrior of truth
Warrior of light
It is I
I'm in here
And have always been

Tune In

The light of your soul shines
No matter what
Be conscious
Close your eyes
Tune in

Drop down into your breath
Sink deeply into your heart
Where all will be revealed
Breath is the crossover
Between spirit and physical reality
Align yourself with spirit
Beauty and openness invites creative
flow
Relax
Everything is ok
Open and expansive
Vulnerable and naked
Exquisitely beautiful
Trust in your capacity to enjoy the ride
Taking risks
Letting go
Naturally flowing through life

Align yourself with spirit
The most exquisite demonstrations of love
Your powerful intentions
Gracefully deliver
Cascading beauty all around you
Patient and persistent

Skillfully guided, carving forms
Blessings from the true creator

I've come to the edge of my comfort zone
Releasing the urge to resist
Spirit is calling me to step beyond
To live in ease, fluidity and grace
Allowing and surrendering any self will
Breathing through any tension
Relaxing, yielding, unfurling
Every moment
Fully present,
Aware,
Conscious
Effortlessly
Breathe

The Starseed Truth

Words are the medicine
That comes through me to heal
Listen to the words
Lose your mind
Listen really listen

Everything on this earth
Contains a medicine to heal
If we just listen and feel
Every whisper
Every cloud passing by
Has the beauty to reveal
The truth with calm consciousness
Just Sit
Breathe,
Feel

Access your multifaceted,
multidimensional being
Calm
Sit
Breathe
In the invisible
As it becomes visible
Integrating ever deeper truths
Truths that call us closer and closer
A miracle of life

We are starseeds biding our time
When we can grow up

From the ground of love
Expanding the beauty
Above and below
Grounded in truth of being love
Tuning into the now

We know exactly what to do
Accelerating the awakening
Of beings sleeping
In their distant ancestral home
Gathering the children
Whose starseeds glow
Bright with blessings of
Mystery evolved
Discovering within
How we all began from one grain
No longer in pain of separation
Collected together in a family

Listen to your story
Heal the past
Reconnect
Share with loving compassion
Ancestral longing coming together
Merging with the mystery of
Divine truth
Expanding beauty above and below
Grounded in the truth of being love
We know exactly
What we must become
Breathing in

The beauty
The simplicity
Release those deeper truths free
Blessings in deep prayer for all beings

Rise up into the being of your body
Play childlike this new cosmic game
Gather in this moment
The medicine of the words reveals
The starseeds truths
Growing free becoming we

Awaken You Are Ready

Awaken you are ready
Now is the time
Your crowning glory is waiting
Let go
Let it flow
Be free
You were meant to be

Awaken you are ready
Being is the portal
Through which you can go
No more worries being all
Let yourself go

Awaken you are ready
Free like a butterfly
Let go
Then you will know
Dropping into your heart
That's only the start

Awaken you are ready
Flowering
Blossoming
Becoming one
Listen to the music deep in your heart
Only you know were thou art

Awaken you are ready
Lover

Beloved
True to ones soul
Guided by the inner divine
Stepping into truth
Serving only the light

Awaken you are ready
Heart broken open
Humbled at ones feet
Take me
Guide me
Show me how to be in this world
Living from truth
The divine wisdom way

Awaken you are ready

Yes, Even You

Trust your inner creative flow
You already know how
You just don't believe it yet
Close your eyes
What do you see?
An impression of that which you were
looking at just before proof that you have
a visual memory

Everyone is creative
Yes, even you
Trust in your ability to see
The next stage of your journey
Surrender to the inner seer
Trust yourself to be free
Free of the judgments and criticisms you
share
While longing to be free
You will see how easy
It is to be Free to follow your
Creative flow
Yes, even you

Trust in your ability to see
The next stage of your journey
Liberated and free from the constraints
those others see
No more to stay small and hide
Close your eyes
Meditate

What do you see?
Believe in your self to carry you through
Others too busy to notice you
Stuck in their story
Not worried about yours
Throw out the rulebook on how it's been
before
Trust yourself
Be free
Yes, even you

Step in to your flow with grace and ease
Trust and be free
Your wildest dreams await
Your creativity
You already have everything you need to
achieve
No fluff
Straight to the point
Everyone is creative
Yes even you

Trust your inner creative flow
You already know how
Close your eyes
What do you see?
Dream and be free

Servant of Peace

Heart songs resonate throughout the land
No more guided by my hand
Living free in harmony
So grateful for each opportunity
Sharing love
At your feet
Awake to life's great mystery
Free
Living humbly
Being what you want me to be

Hearing your call
Forever your servant of peace
Great warrior spirit
My body
My soul
I am yours
Shamanic lifestyle is the way
Giving thanks for each and every day
In deepest gratitude for all that is
Freedom comes from giving in
Surrendering to the light within

Oneness

The tender heart beckons
Love for all
Every event an opportunity to deepen
our practice
Every event specifically designed to
awaken our senses
Feeling ever deeply into our being
Silence allows the inner voice to be heard
The more we are still the louder the sound
Feeling into the divine plan

Freedom of will, no longer our goal
Oneness, sparkling in every action
Deeper remembering of our true song
Whispering, guiding, loves true path
Totally surrendered into heart song

Living in peace and harmony
No longer judging heart song or ego's
trickery
Listening to truth we become free
Living deeper in peace and harmony

No more running from my shadow
Facing each day strong in my heart
Great spirit I surrender to the truth of
your light
Guiding me with your great insight
Transmuting pain into loves warrior
light

Everything perfect
This moment in time

Inner Spark

We are all made of stardust
We all have the inner yearning to
Be more, do more and have more
Most people strive every day to fulfill
The dreams of another
Look inside for the inner spark calling
That inspires and guides you
It's patiently waiting for your attention
You've heard it many times before
No longer ignore it
Fill it with all your heart
Let love guide you to the place
Where you spark
The divine imagination in others
To help wake them up from the dark
Hear your calling every night and day
No longer resisting the pull of the divine
Filled with love and joy in your heart
You'll inspire others to awaken
To their true calling

Divine Calling

Words can be medicine sent to heal
Powerful arrows of our will
The perfect combination for awakening
the spirit within
Listening to the calling deep inside
Voices teaching you to abide
Living fully in peace and harmony
Journeying to the center of your soul
You have always been
Ohm mane pad me hum
Love is the one

The one true thread binding us all
Feminine intuition combining
With the masculine will
Bringing dreams for humanity to fruition
Always in the deepest faith
Words to uplift and inspire
The star seed truth we all contain
So many choices
Listen deeply to your heart
Follow your truth
In the depths of your being is
The giant awakening
To the calling of ones inner most being
Listen
Trust
Follow your divine calling

Note: I dedicate this last poem to divine brother ji, Gabriel Icka Martinez who inspired these words while listening to his account of his recent trip to India. It feels like a prayer giving thanks for the power of water to uplift all of humanity. I feel so blessed that you inspire me daily to live in my truth and to share these words with the world.

Divine Being

Home in my body cleansed by the waters
No more separation
All is one
Divine inclusion
Other worldly technology
Beyond religion
Beyond all busllshit
All of it out

The magic of lineage
To manifest reality
The fire burning
Intensely melting away
All that comforts me
To expose the truth of
All that is within

Meditation the key
To ancient wisdom divine
Defending the purity of source
Let go of limitations
Confidently move forward
Express yourself

Say it
Be free

Finally I sincerely hope that you have enjoyed this collection of poems and that they bring you deep comfort in those moments when you are learning to trust. Just let go and know that you are always being taken care of. I'm always happy to receive your story and help you find ways to integrate it in a useful and sustainable way. Because it is my sincere belief that: Every event is an opportunity to deepen our practice of consciously accepting each part of ourselves, even the parts we may have unconsciously disowned and projected onto others.

Every event is an opportunity to become consciously aware of every action that causes harm so we can correct it.

Of consciously evolving into the person we were always destined to be, full of love, light, compassion and joy.

Living in right action, right relationship and not causing harm to the earth or other beings.

Donna regularly facilitates events to help individuals to connect with their own inner divine spark, please check her website for further information and if you'd like to get in touch and share your insights from reading this poetry.

Giving thanks to the divine source of greatest wisdom teachers.

Aho Mitakuye Oasin, For ALL our relations

70887681R00040

Made in the USA
Columbia, SC
16 May 2017